SMALL GROUP MINISTRIES

Where two or three are gathered

By Diana L. Hynson
General Board of Discipleship

SMALL GROUP MINISTRIES

Copyright © 2004 by Cokesbury

This book is printed on acid-free paper.

ISBN 0-687-00070-X

MANUFACTURED IN THE UNITED STATES OF AMERICA

CONTENTS

Our Identity, Call, and Mission

Y ou are so important to the life of the Christian church! You have consented to be among a great and long line of people who have shared the faith and led others in the work of Jesus Christ. We have the church only because over the millennia people like you have caught the vision of God's kingdom and have claimed a place in the faith community to extend God's love to others. You have been called and have committed your unique passions, gifts, and abilities in a position of leadership, and this guide will help you understand some of the elements of that ministry and how it fits within the mission of your church and of The United Methodist Church.

"The mission of the Church is to make disciples of Jesus Christ. Local churches provide the most significant arena through which disciple-making occurs" (*The Book of Discipline of The United Methodist Church, 2004,* ¶120). The church is not only local but also global, and it is for everyone. Our church has an organizational structure through which we work, but it is a living organism as well. Each person is called to ministry by virtue of his or her baptism, and that ministry takes place in all aspects of daily life, not just within the walls of the church. Our *Book of Discipline* describes our mission to proclaim the gospel and to welcome people into the body of Christ, to lead people to a commitment to God through Jesus Christ, to nurture them in Christian living by various means of grace, and to send them into the world as agents of Jesus Christ (¶121). Thus, through you—and many other Christians—this very relational mission continues. (The *Discipline* explains the ministry of all Christians and the essence of servant ministry and leadership in ¶¶125–137.)

Essential Leadership Functions

Five functions of leadership are essential to strengthen and support the ministry of the church: identifying and supporting leaders as spiritual leaders, discovering current reality, naming shared vision, developing action plans, and monitoring the journey. This Guideline will help you identify these elements and set a course for ministry.

Lead in the Spirit

Each leader is a spiritual leader and has the opportunity to model spiritual maturity and discipline. John Wesley referred to the disciplines that cultivate a relationship with God as the "means of grace" and suggested several means: prayer, Bible study, fasting, public and private worship, Christian conversation, and acts of mercy. Local church leaders are strongly encouraged to identify their own spiritual practices, cultivate new ones as they grow in their own faith, and model and encourage these practices among their ministry team participants.

Discover Current Reality

"The way things are" is your current reality. How you organize, who does what, how bills get paid and plans get made are all building blocks of your current reality. Spend time with people who have been in this ministry and with your committee members to assess their view of how things are. Use "Christian conversation," one of the means of grace, not only to talk to others openly about their understanding of current reality but also to listen for the voice of God regarding your area of ministry.

Name Shared Vision

"The way things are" is only a prelude to "the way you want things to be." When the church is truly of God, it is the way God would envision it to be. Spend time with your committee and with other leaders in the church to discern the best and most faithful future you can imagine. How can you together identify your role and place in a faithful community that extends itself in its fourfold mission of reaching out and receiving people in the name of God, relating people to God, nurturing them in Christ and Christian living, and sending them forth as ministers into the world? Examine your committee's role and its place in that big picture and try to see yourselves as God's agents of grace and love.

Develop Action Plans

How do you get from here (your current reality) to there (your shared vision)? As a leader, one of your tasks is to hold in view both what is and what is hoped for so that you can build bridges to the future. These bridges are the interim goals and the action plans needed to accomplish the goals that will make your vision a reality. Remember that God may open up many (or different) avenues to that future, so be flexible and open to setting new goals and accepting new challenges. Action plans that describe how to meet interim goals should be specific, measurable, and attainable. While it is faithful to allow for the wondrous work of God in setting out bold plans, balance that boldness with realism. You and your committee will find information and tips here on developing and implementing the shared vision, the goals toward that vision, and the specific action plans that will accomplish the goals.

Monitor the Journey

A fifth responsibility of leaders is to keep an eye on how things are going. Setbacks will surely occur, but effective leaders keep moving toward their envisioned future. Not only will you monitor the progress of your committee's action plans to a faithful future but you will also be called to evaluate them in light of the ministry of the rest of the church. Immerse yourself and your plans in God's love and care. Voices from the congregation (both pro and con) may be the nudging of God to shift direction, rethink or plan, or move ahead boldly and without fear. Faithful leaders are attentive to the discernment of the congregation and to the heart of God in fulfilling the mission of the church.

The Role of the Small Group Ministries Leader

All churches have small groups, even if they are not identified as part of the "small group ministries." You have accepted the role of leader or coordinator of small groups or small group ministries, which means that you will be a small group leader yourself.

In this role, you may work with others to coordinate the existing small groups and leaders (which makes you a small group leader), identify what other groups may be needed, and help start and nurture those groups. You will help recruit persons with a passion for small groups and persons representing the composition of the congregation—youth, young adults, middle adults, older adults, new Christians, mature Christians, and so on—to be on the Small Group Ministry Team. You may occasionally be called upon to facilitate the closing or ending of groups. Your task is to coordinate groups, not to lead all the groups. You may work with the church council and pastor to identify the congregational needs that will suggest what groups you need to start (or end).

What Is Small Group Ministries?

The primary purpose of small groups is faith formation and disciple making. Regardless of their stated identity, task, and purpose, small groups are places within which their members can grow spiritually and be equipped for their own ministry in day-to-day life, whatever that ministry may be.

When we speak of small group ministry, we may think of a collection of groups within which we can integrate and connect all our church members and constituents to help them have a sense of belonging to the larger congregation. In that context, many of the groups' purposes would be relational, social, recreational, or interest-based. It is vital to help people in the congregation feel they are welcome, known, valued, needed, and cared for. The larger the church, the more intentional must the leadership be in helping people have a place and means of connection. Yet small group ministries is more than that.

What Are Small Groups?

Every church has small groups. No matter how small the church, there is probably some smaller unit within: a Sunday school class, a women's group, or a planning committee for an annual fund-raiser, for example.

Small groups are places where persons gather on a regular basis for study, worship, prayer, fellowship, and accountability. Persons in small groups are engaged in relevant, meaningful discussions. All persons in a small group accept that they have a role and a responsibility for being active participants in the group. Small groups extend hospitality to newcomers by reaching out to others and intentionally incorporating them into the life of the group.

Churches also have essential ministry and task groups required by *The Book of Discipline of The United Methodist Church* that fall in the broad categories of administration, leader development, witness, outreach, and nurture, which include numerous groups: all the committees, study and fellowship groups, devotional groups, caregiving ministries, special interest or fellowship groups, local and global missions groups, and so on. All of these groups make up a discipleship system in your church, within which persons are nurtured in the faith and formed as disciples. As the small group ministries coordinator, you (along with other leaders) have a stake in assessing the health, vitality, and purpose of existing groups so that you can determine what new groups may be needed and which groups under your care need more guidance and support.

Not all of these groups, however, are small. The board of trustees, for example, is limited to nine persons, but you could have a forty-member Sunday school class or a sixty-three-member choir. So, what do we mean by "small"?

"Small" means three to perhaps fifteen members. Depending on the purpose of the group, there is an optimal number for membership. Groups tend to settle into that number; five to seven in learning and decision-making groups and eight to twelve for fellowship and project groups. Much larger groups may find it helpful to form smaller cells within the whole so that participants can more easily establish a sense of acquaintance and trust with each other. Other large groups may choose to divide and multiply by sending out members to birth new groups.

The Value of Small Groups

Through small groups, regardless of their stated task or purpose, you have the best opportunity for faith formation and disciple making. What happens in small groups that leads its participants to grow and mature in their faith and in the use of their gifts for discipleship?

- **A sense of meaning and belonging.** The best way to welcome people into the life of the whole church is to introduce them to a small group. In that setting, members have a safe place within which to experience themselves as a part of the group, the church, the community, and the household of God. They find meaning or purpose when both their contributions and needs are valued and taken seriously.

- **Trust and intimacy.** Groups that are small provide a better arena than larger groups within which to establish a sense of trust and an appropriate level of intimacy. Almost all people have some yearning for a personal connection. As members of the body of Christ, we share our lives and stories, our dreams and hopes, our needs and wounds—but only when we feel safe. Groups that have gone through their formation stage move to a stage of trust. Members have abided with each other long enough to get acquainted, to see if their mutual covenant is being kept, and to establish a comfort level in communication. When the appropriate level of intimacy has been achieved (which may be different for different members), then persons are ready to risk the vulnerability with each other that will allow them to grow spiritually.

- **Support and accountability.** The willingness to be vulnerable does not come, though, without appropriate support and accountability. Within the structure of a small group, where everyone is known and has established a comfortable level of trust, members can both rely on the support and kindness of the other members to care for and about them and also to tolerate with grace an honest assessment of where they fall short.

All small groups will establish some form of covenant, even if it is unspoken, unwritten, or unconscious. Group leaders will benefit more from a mindful approach to a covenant; that is, a statement and vision of how group members relate to one another. When expectations are clear and mutually determined, there is a solid basis both for support (because all have agreed on how to care for each other) and for accountability (because all know what to expect of and from each other).

- **Community and hospitality.** We can't be Christians by ourselves; we need a community, which is one of the beneficial by-products of a healthy small group. Our small groups cannot just be "stand alone" cells within the body of Christ; they are necessary parts for the function of the whole. Each small group is a kind of "little church" within the community of the whole church—and that "whole" local church is just one tiny but vital part of the universal church of Jesus Christ.

Within that community, everyone is called to the same radical hospitality that Jesus extended to all persons, including those toward whom we feel the least affinity or least need to extend hospitality. There are many fine and appropriate gestures of hospitality: providing safe space, offering food or other comforts, being sure each person is introduced and included, and so on. But in the final analysis, hospitality is much more than good hosting and welcoming skills; it is a part of our being and innate doing. How do we welcome the "stranger and sojourner," the person who is "marginal" or even regarded as "enemy" or "unlovable"? These are the persons to whom Jesus offered his gracious preference, and small group members are called to do no less.

A System of Faith Formation and Disciple Making

The *Book of Discipline* indicates that every local church has the same mission or "primary task": to make disciples, which is described as a process with four intertwined aspects that together achieve one task. The church reaches out both to its own members and also to the community to invite and receive persons into the body of Christ. Church members and leaders are responsible for helping to provide a place wherein persons can come to know God and have a relationship through the practice of the means of grace: worship, devotional life, study of the Scriptures, fasting and abstinence, prayer, Communion, the ministry of the Word, and Christian conferencing. (See also the section "Spiritual Leadership" on page 17). Further more the church helps to equip those persons to discern their gifts for ministry both within the church and out in the community or wider setting; that is, to become disciples. This equipping enables members to live out their baptismal vows in the community and world and to use their gifts to reach out to others in the name of Jesus Christ.

These four aspects of faith formation and disciple making must operate together, although some groups will emphasize one aspect more than others. At some level for everyone in the church, the primary task is engaged by the groups in the church as vital and complementary partners in ministry. As a very simplistic example, the evangelism committee and the *Witness* group members have a major stake in reaching out and receiving persons. A new members class and *Companions in Christ* group have a significant role in helping persons cultivate their relationship to God through Jesus Christ. A DISCIPLE Bible study group, faith sharing group, or Volunteers in Mission team may help persons claim their gifts for ministry and to grow as disciples. The community advocacy group, *Steward* class, or Mother's Day Out team help nurture persons as they take their gifts outward in ministry to the life of the community. However, even if one aspect of the Primary Task is emphasized by a particular group, that group will ideally have the whole task as a framework within which they work.

Rather than each small group within the church simply "doing its own thing" without regard for what the other groups are doing, group leaders and members see how all the groups in the church interact to form this system of faith formation and disciple making that fulfills the primary task. This awareness promotes a strong synergy—the dynamism that allows the whole to be more than a sum of its parts. The church is a living organism (a system) that breathes life and promotes spiritual health and wholeness because it is Christ-centered, not merely church-centered. As the small group ministry coordinator, one of your roles is to teach and interpret this holistic approach to small group life together and to help create and maintain this small group system of faith formation and disciple making.

The Biblical/Theological Grounding

Scripture and tradition support our life together in small groups. This brief section will suffice to illustrate how.

A Biblical Witness

God called Abraham to be the "father of many nations," and the Hebrew Scriptures (or Old Testament) give lengthy witness to the activity of God within the tribes and clans of the Hebrew people. Jesus called his disciples, including a band of twelve who formed an "inner circle" but who certainly worked with many others in groups and teams to spread the word. The disciples gathered together and received a great promise from the risen Lord to be among them, including after the Crucifixion and Resurrection: "Where two or three are gathered in my name, I am there among [you]" (Matthew 18:20), and "Remember, I am with you always, to the end of the age" (28:20).

Acts 2

Empowered by these and other promises, the disciples carried on. The story of the first Pentecost is often called the "birthday of the church." In Acts 2, we see the visitation of the Holy Spirit in a powerful demonstration of group solidarity: each of the visiting pilgrims heard his language being spoken by the Galilean disciples who by all accounts would not have had that linguistic skill otherwise. The sense of togetherness and awe at the power of God created numerous converts that day. We are told that thousands of people responded to this word of grace. This new faith community shared their possessions and goods equitably, worshiped and learned together, and enjoyed table fellowship with each other and a rapport with the rest of the community. Their model and God's love were compelling enough for the community to grow "day by day" (see Acts 2:41-47).

These passages confirm for us that we are called as a people of God to be in relationship with each other and with God, that we have a requirement and process by which we can both be supported and held accountable in community, and that there are models for our life together that are based on the shared practice of the means of grace.

Society, Class, and Band

We "fast-forward" several centuries to note that part of the genius of John Wesley was his appreciation of the small group as a place of faith formation and disciple making. He instituted his own system of groups in establishing the society, classes, and bands.

The society meeting was created for the many persons who had experienced a spiritual renewal or transformation during the religious revival sweeping England in the eighteenth century. Wesley was closely associated with two of these Christian societies in particular, which came under his leadership. Open to all who had simply "a desire to flee from the wrath to come, and to be saved from their sins" and to live as forgiven and reconciled Christians, the societies were places of religious support, faith development, and help in living out their religious convictions in their day-to-day lives.

Subgroupings were also formed within the societies for related, but slightly different purposes. The bands, same gender groups of five to ten persons, gathered to provide mutual support and accountability, confession, and Christian conversation as the band members assisted each other in their spiritual growth. The classes, mixed groups of about twelve to twenty, were assigned according to their proximity to each other, and the focus was primarily pastoral and instructional.

As the groups developed, it became clear that all of them offered a tremendous opportunity for Christian formation. Members became better acquainted, whether in groups of all men, all women, or mixed groups; they supported one another; they offered up in some way their own need for accountability and opportunities for growth; they learned more about the faith; and they gained skills and honed gifts for living as faithful disciples in the midst of their everyday lives. One current offering within your small group system could be the Covenant Discipleship group modeled on Wesley's class meeting. (See Resources for Covenant Discipleship resources.)

What Is My Job?

You may be thinking by now, *"Enough theory. What am I supposed to do?"* That's a very good question. In short, as the leader of a small group ministry, you relate to the leaders of existing and new groups, which may include cooperating and coordinating with the pastor and chairperson of the church council, so that the **group life** is healthy, vital, and fulfilling its part of the primary task. You may strongly consider recruiting a ministry team that keeps the vision of small groups before the congregation, establishes new groups, equips persons as leaders, and provides a structure of support for small group leaders. *While this Guideline is addressed to you, the work is shared by your ministry team, if you have one.* You and your ministry team will:

- provide guidance for group leaders to identify and articulate their biblical/theological reason for being

- help current group leaders assess how well they and their group fulfill their part of the primary task

- help current group leaders understand the value and purpose of a systematic approach to small groups and small group ministry so that they achieve the synergy mentioned earlier

- recruit, equip, and nurture small group leaders

- plan and start new groups as needed and end groups when necessary.

Assess Existing Groups

The chart on page 13 will provide a good beginning place to explain to others how the group system in your church could be shaped. But first, some caveats.

- Each church is unique, so this picture cannot begin to capture the whole of what your church is. It is merely suggestive of groups you may have.

- The picture is flat and one-dimensional, but it attempts to portray a multi-layered, dynamic reality. You will have to use your imagination!

- The lines between each ministry category are soft and seldom sharply defined. As you try to decide where to place the existing groups in your church in the schema presented, hardly anything will fit neatly.

- This is only one way to picture the system of groups in your church, and another will be suggested as well.

Small Group System and Visioning

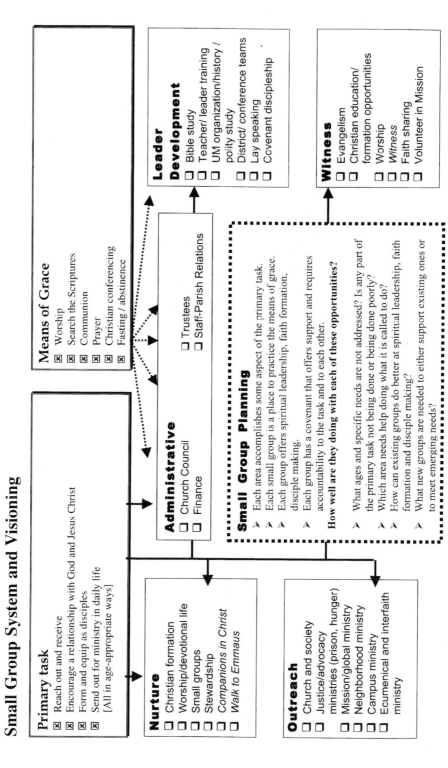

Primary task
- ☒ Reach out and receive
- ☒ Encourage a relationship with God and Jesus Christ
- ☒ Form and equip as disciples
- ☒ Send out for ministry in daily life
  [All in age-appropriate ways]

Means of Grace
- ☒ Worship
- ☒ Search the Scriptures
- ☒ Communion
- ☒ Prayer
- ☒ Christian conferencing
- ☒ Fasting / abstinence

Leader Development
- ☐ Bible study
- ☐ Teacher/ leader training
- ☐ UM organization/history / polity study
- ☐ District/ conference teams
- ☐ Lay speaking
- ☐ Covenant discipleship

Witness
- ☐ Evangelism
- ☐ Christian education/ formation opportunities
- ☐ Worship
- ☐ *Witness*
- ☐ Faith sharing
- ☐ Volunteer in Mission

Administrative
- ☐ Church Council
- ☐ Finance
- ☐ Trustees
- ☐ Staff-Parish Relations

Small Group Planning
- ⋀ Each area accomplishes some aspect of the primary task.
- ⋀ Each small group is a place to practice the means of grace.
- ⋀ Each group offers spiritual leadership, faith formation, disciple making.
- ⋀ Each group has a covenant that offers support and requires accountability to the task and to each other.

How well are they doing with each of these opportunities?

- ⋀ What ages and specific needs are not addressed? Is any part of the primary task not being done or being done poorly?
- ⋀ Which area needs help doing what it is called to do?
- ⋀ How can existing groups do better at spiritual leadership, faith formation and disciple making?
- ⋀ What new groups are needed to either support existing ones or to meet emerging needs?

Nurture
- ☐ Christian formation
- ☐ Worship/devotional life
- ☐ Small groups
- ☐ Stewardship
- ☐ *Companions in Christ*
- ☐ *Walk to Emmaus*

Outreach
- ☐ Church and society
- ☐ Justice/advocacy ministries (prison, hunger)
- ☐ Mission/global ministry
- ☐ Neighborhood ministry
- ☐ Campus ministry
- ☐ Ecumenical and interfaith ministry

The primary task of every church is to make disciples, and disciples are strengthened and empowered in their faith formation and service by practicing the means of grace. Thus, we see the arrows flowing from "Primary Task" and "Means of Grace" into each of the ministry areas.

As you think about your church, identify the ministry categories (shown on the chart as Nurture, Outreach, Administrative, Leader Development, and Witness, which the *Book of Discipline* requires). Then list ALL the groups, formal and informal, in your church. You may not even know about all the groups; in any case, consider asking several other leaders and the pastor to contribute to the list. *(This entire process would be a very helpful exercise for the church council and is best done at least with the leaders of the individual groups, even if you meet with only one or a few at a time. You may also do this as a solitary activity first, just to be mindful of your own experience and observations. You may bring objectivity that group members and leaders do not see in the same way from the inside.)*

Determine where those groups would fit within the ministry categories, remembering that many will have a "foot in several camps." You can either decide what the major function is and list a group once or acknowledge the multi-faceted nature of the group and list it everywhere it fits. Group members and leaders may prefer to self-identify, however.

How, and how well, does the group fulfill the primary task? Look at the group as it is now and also imagine that the group is working at its healthiest and most effective level. Determine with the actual group how the members and their leader understand their task and responsibility in view of the church's mission. Best to let the group articulate this themselves, if possible, while you privately assess what you think as well.

What means of grace are practiced there and to what effect? As you take inventory, you will particularly need to be a facilitator and a partner, not a judge or critic. You may need to help group leaders become familiar with how to practice and help their group members practice the means of grace. For some groups this will come more easily than for others, and it may take time to establish. Christian spiritual practices are valuable and appropriate for every group, including, for example, administrative groups or others that are primarily task-oriented. In any case, remember that this is a vision of a way to be together and should be invitational, never coercive.

As members of the body of Christ, group members have the opportunity and the responsibility to care for and about each other as they fulfill the functions of their office. Any gathering of any group can begin or end with prayer and include at least a brief time of devotion or reflection on a relevant Bible passage. Christian conferencing, speaking with a discerning ear to the voice of God in the conversation, is well-employed in any meeting or group setting and may be particularly helpful if group members are at an impasse or are experiencing conflict, for example. As an example of the practice of fasting, group members may agree to take a "fast" from operating out of unchecked assumptions or may abstain from evaluation of any idea or proposal until it has had a full hearing. Even in a "business" oriented ministry group, the means of grace are good business that leads to a deeper relationship with God.

How well do the group leaders and members understand their stated task, or reason for being, and how they fit into the overall picture of the church's life and ministry? As groups hone their sense of identity and recognize how they fulfill the primary task, they move the church closer to vitality. As they understand how the other groups work in a complementary way, they move the church closer to a dynamic and synergistic system. Seeing their own vital and cooperative role deflects the narrow approach of isolation in "my little group to do my thing," and it expands their effectiveness by helping to eliminate the need for competition and "turf battles." Everyone is on the same side, and everyone has a vital role to play.

How comprehensive is the group system across the life span? Small groups include people of all ages, particularly for Christian education and formation, through the church school, after-school ministries, youth and young adult ministries, and covenant groups for children and young people (such as Sprouts and Chrysalis). While we may think mainly about new groups for adults, faith formation and disciple making can start at birth. If we neglect these matters with our children and youth, we will soon have very few adult disciples!

Assessment tools are available to help you. See the Small Group Ministries links at the General Board of Discipleship web site (www.gbod.org/smallgroup/seminars).

Another View of the Small Group System

You may have another way to categorize or define small groups and their purposes. One further suggestion is to focus on three or four primary categories or characteristics, such as disciple making, faith formation, task orientation, and fellowship, for example, though many groups will include more than one of those foci. As groups self-identify according to a principle category, they may also assess how well they meet the needs of people across the faith spectrum, from the curious to the mature in faith.

Another measure or point of assessment for groups is how well they involve the age span of the church. The primary task is for the entire church, not just the adults, so group leaders will need to be aware of how well groups attend to the needs of children and youth and their faith development. A further step may be to identify all the resources currently in use or available and categorize them as well, indicating which are for particular task groups, for faith development (and at what level of maturity), for discernment of gifts for discipleship, and so on. The length of the study or development resource should also be considered; introductory materials are often shorter (perhaps six weeks) than those intended for more "seasoned" participants (such as the twenty-eight plus week materials in the DISCIPLE or *Companions in Christ* series).

Educate Group Leaders

Not all group leaders will have this portrait of how the small groups in the church form a system. Some may be content to operate in a fairly solitary fashion and not bother with all that "synergy stuff." Some will not be interested in or see the relevance of adding the practice of the means of grace to whatever they already do. This may be a matter of unfamiliarity; many will simply not have thought of it. Others may be resistant, even hostile to the idea.

Your role as the leader or coordinator of small group ministry will be to introduce, educate, and coach the leaders to see a bigger picture. Your role is NOT to insist that leaders have to "get with the program" in a way that feels alien or intimidating to them but to help broaden their view to embrace this larger picture if it is new to them. This may take some time.

Identify the Biblical/Theological Grounding of Groups

As we suggested earlier, each group should have some understanding of what its biblical and theological grounding is and be able to articulate it. This is not difficult; we just don't usually take the time or make the effort. Encourage group leaders and the group members to spend some time discerning this.

How is this done? First, think about the theological concepts that apply to community and church life, for example: fellowship of the "saints," making disciples, building up the community of faith, offering grace and hospitality, forgiveness and reconciliation, discerning God's will, witnessing to God's presence, practicing the means of grace, and so on. Then review the mission, task, or purpose of the group. How does it fit with the primary task of the church? How does it fit with what we know, believe, and demonstrate about God and our relationship with God?

In addition, help group leaders identify at least one Scripture passage that supplies their own "marching orders." If this seems a mystery, first brainstorm a number of ideas about what the group does (or review the group's mission statement), then search a topical Bible concordance. If you have a fragment of a Bible verse, a word-oriented concordance will help. Look up the passages you discover and do a bit of study to ensure that you understand the context (rather than forcing a few verses or words out of context to fit). Test the passage with the group members and suggest that they formulate a group mission statement if they don't already have one. The mission statement must cohere with the primary task of the church, and again, the group members should then have a clear understanding of how they fit in with and complement the other groups in the church.

Equip and Nurture Group Leaders

Once the assessment phase is completed, (though not for all time; you'll need to do this periodically), you get to the next core responsibility of your task as coordinator. Ideally, leaders are prepared, trained, equipped, or oriented before they assume a leadership position, but that is not always so. Keep leaders fresh and interested through ongoing nurture and continuing education. Leaders who are put in place and then ignored will be good candidates for burnout or discouragement. Following the biblical and theological understanding and the importance of faith formation and disciple making, a third element for leader development is in helping leaders understand that they are spiritual leaders, regardless of the purpose or task of the group.

Spiritual Leadership

Spiritual leadership is easier than you may think! As the coordinator, you are a spiritual leader for your ministry team, and those team members are to be spiritual leaders within the small groups for which they have responsibility. The central element of spiritual leadership within your small group system is to help the leaders remain Christ-centered and to recall the biblical and theological purpose of their groups. Whatever else you do in the group, the group must be of God if it is considered a part of the church's ministry. Keep your eye on the main thing.

Practicing the means of grace within the group is another aspect of spiritual leadership. Again, this is probably easier than you think. Remember the third stanza of "There Is a Balm in Gilead" (375, *The United Methodist Hymnal*): "If you can't preach like Peter, if you can't pray like Paul, just tell the love of Jesus…." Being a spiritual leader is not the same as being a "spiritual giant" whose level of faithfulness and personal piety seem out of reach for most of us. Beginning and ending your time together with a brief prayer or devotional time, for example, is a means of bringing persons in your group closer to God and of being more aligned with God's will. And that is all the means of grace are—ways that help us cultivate a relationship with God. Those prayers don't have to be spontaneous, either. There are countless books and other resources (including the *Hymnal*) that offer fine devotional materials.

One other means of grace is Holy Communion, which you could observe with the help of an ordained member of the church staff to consecrate the elements. However, sharing in table fellowship with any sort of meal is also a sacramental act, and a simple blessing is sufficient. Fasting or abstinence is also a means of grace, and it doesn't have to be abstention from food. Fasting is sometimes combined with an outward offering. We give up something in order to give out something or give in to something. Perhaps you will lead the group in a fast from negativity so that you can take on new ideas or receive new members with an open heart and mind.

Christian conferencing, or speaking together to try to discern God's spirit and will, is an important means of grace for group life. Any time you need to make a decision, sort out conflicting viewpoints, consider options, or order priorities in a group that is Christ-centered, do some intentional searching out of God's will. Ask yourselves, *"What would Jesus do?"* as an introductory question for Christian conferencing. Perhaps a good second question is, "What would Jesus never do in such a circumstance?" That may be a helpful reminder (when we fall into temptation!) that gossip, acrimony, unforgiveness, injustice, and highhandedness have no place in small group life.

Corporate worship and personal devotions may not seem obvious for small group life; it's what we do either privately or all together. Small group members can and should be led on occasion in devotional time together to help keep the group Christ-centered. In addition, small group leaders who are seen attending worship model faithfulness, as well as spiritual maturity and discipline, for others. As a leader in the church, it is crucial for you to attend worship and to encourage other small group leaders to do the same.

Searching the Scriptures is yet another means of grace. You will have already helped other small group leaders identify scriptural "marching orders" so that they can place their small group life and ministry in a biblical and theological context. At least occasional Bible study during the group life is one more avenue of spiritually nurturing your leaders (and modeling for them). Every group has a responsibility for faith formation and disciple making. Familiarity with Scripture and knowing how to make spiritual meaning from it enhance your leaders and their group life.

Continuing Education

Your small group leaders have a multitude of different tasks and purposes. Some will be responsible for fellowship groups, others for devotional groups, study groups, task groups, administrative groups, and so on. While there are overlapping training needs for all small group leaders, obviously they also need ongoing educational opportunities that are specific to what they do. Your task as the coordinator of small groups and small group leaders is to look for and plan for these opportunities.

This set of Guidelines includes a workshop model, "Guide to the Guidelines," to help all the church leaders become oriented to their ministry area by using their specific volume in the Guidelines. There is an online learning center approach for teachers and other education leaders to use the series *What Every Teacher Needs to Know About....* Other specific continuing education opportunities for specific leaders may be available online or in print. (Check the resource listing at the end of the Guideline for possible sources, including people who can come to you to offer training. Remember to check with your district and conference for local options and resource persons.)

What other educational helps might be useful? Consider finding or preparing an occasional workshop on some aspect of group life such as: "Understanding Group Dynamics," "Recognizing Groups as Places of Faith Formation and Transformation," "Leading Meetings," "Training Effective Leaders" or "Conflict Resolution and Reconciliation." The General Board of Discipleship offers small group ministry seminars that can be tailored to the needs of the host group. (See Resources, page 32, or go to www.gbod.org/smallgroup/seminars).

Mentoring, Coaching, Teaching, Facilitating

One great temptation or pressure you may encounter as a leader of group leaders is to try to fix things when there is a problem. Resist this urge. This is not to say that you have no part to play in finding a solution, but that is different from fixing.

In small group life, most problems have to do with differences in how we think, what values we hold, what expectations we foster, what relationships we have, what cultural or social patterns we find familiar (or unfamiliar), what models of power we find comfortable, and so on. These are personal, sometimes emotional, "adaptive" issues. If a difficulty arises, we often try to fix it by changing a meeting place or time, imposing a new rule or abandoning a previous one, or changing leaders or resources (technical solutions). A logical or process-oriented response to a personal or emotional issue generally misses the point and does not work. We miss the real issues and fail to find a suitable, durable solution.

When persons in the throes of an adaptive problem come to you for help, they may be seeking a technical fix with you acting as the "heavy." Be careful. This is where you decide what sort of help is the most useful: mentoring, coaching, teaching, or facilitating. Not only can you provide assistance but you can also model a healthy process for other leaders to work out their own issues.

In **mentoring**, an experienced leader (who doesn't have to be you) is paired with a less experienced leader. Ideally in your small group life, a successor to the group leader will emerge from the group after having had the chance to witness and practice appropriate leadership skills. The "apprentice" leader will already understand (or come to understand) the group purpose, history, goals, dynamics, customs, values, and idiosyncrasies. Passing the torch to a mentored colleague is a gift to the group. You don't have to be the mentor, but you can participate in arranging for these leadership pairings and in checking on those relationships periodically.

In other situations, groups may benefit from **coaching**, which is not counseling, intervention, fixing, or mentoring. Most often a good coach will not so much introduce new information or skills but rather will draw out from the coached leader what he or she already has within. (If what is needed is not already within, another kind of facilitation may be necessary.) A good coach is a guide to helping the coached leader recognize his or her own issues, barriers, strengths, desires, and so on and how to pursue them.

Teachers will impart new content and help students learn how to transform data into information that is useful and retrievable. In order to "stick," content must touch us on an emotional level ("this means something" or "this offers some value to me") and have a relationship to something that already makes sense. Good teachers will help make those associations. You may be called upon to teach new skills or to help find another way for those skills to be learned, perhaps through district, conference, or denominational training events.

A **facilitator** helps others make things happen. You may be called upon to be the "process person," someone who will run interference for a group life issue with the trustees if there are space issues, for example, or who will bring conflicted parties to the table to discuss whatever ails them. The facilitator does not fix the issue but enables others to handle their own issues. This allows the facilitator to observe where a process is flowing, where (and why and how), it gets bogged down, and then to establish the next steps toward solving an impasse or making a decision.

Starting New Groups

After you and the various group leaders have assessed the current reality of group life in your church, you and your ministry team can continue to work with current leaders to help ensure that groups are fulfilling the primary task and practicing the means of grace. Then you may turn your attention to the creation of new groups. The assessment tools presented earlier will help you identify the small groups you have and what groups you need.

Planning for New Groups

Remember that small group life and ministry extends beyond adults. A church that does not attend to helping children and youth learn to be faithful disciples will be empty before too long. Responsibility for children's and youth ministry falls elsewhere, but your participation on the church council or other planning arenas allows you to advocate for small group ministry for all ages.

How do we know what groups to start? First, what groups are your church members or community residents asking for? What groups have others offered to start? What has the church council set as a priority that can be facilitated by a new group? What trends are emerging in the church that lend themselves to a group response?

Consider those and other questions as you plan.

- **What people are missing in our small group life?** (specific people, age groupings, persons who attend only worship, young couples or young adults, singles)

- **What life issues or special interests may need to be addressed and at what age level?** (divorce or grief recovery, trauma, single parenting, blending families, interracial or intercultural relationships, health and wellness, self-help or Anon groups, economic or debt recovery, unemployment, networking, and resume writing)

- **What new social outlets may be beneficial for persons across the age spectrum** (home, retirement home, nursing home social groups, parent or caregiver day out, church newcomers, intercultural awareness, and recreation groups)

- **What missional activities are needed in the community that are not addressed or are not adequately addressed?** (food pantry, clothing outlet, English language training, literacy education, community advocacy for senior adults or children, after school or preschool programming, tutoring)

- **What new devotional or study groups (short- or long-term) will reach persons not already engaged?** (DISCIPLE, *Companions in Christ, Witness, Christian Believer, Steward*, short-term Sunday or mid-week study, Fourth Day Emmaus groups, spiritual direction or discernment groups, faith-meets-life discussion group, book study.) Are groups balanced so that there are offerings for beginning Christians and mature Christians, leaders, and so on?

- **What recreational activities could meet fellowship needs, especially to cultivate a sense of belonging?** (potluck or other dinners, quilting or sewing group, cooperative and healthy competitive sports teams, game night, exercise class, classes for various arts)

- **What short-term or occasional projects need a team to be accomplished,** not only for the church but perhaps also for needy members or community residents? (clean up day, maintenance and repair jobs, snow shoveling or leaf raking, grass cutting, babysitting services, fundraisers)

- **What short-term professional services could be offered** by members or friends of the congregation to meet special, occasional, unaffordable needs? (financial or debt-recovery counseling, will preparation, driving test tutoring, caregiver respite, training for home caregiving, anger management, communication skills, conflict resolution skills, art or craft therapy)

- **What community-oriented groups might be needed?** (school board, local business advocacy, neighborhood organizing, community clean up, historic building or district reclamation, "Shalom zones")

- **What on-going groups in the community could use your space** and thereby accommodate church members? (Scouts and other youth- or children-serving agencies, anonymous groups, Christian or ecumenical or interfaith-oriented groups)

- **What existing small groups might want to add a service or missional dimension** to what they already do? (Remember that children may need special guidance and supervision, but they love to help others.)

- **On occasion, geographical groups may make sense,** especially if they are community or neighborhood oriented.

Why People Join Groups

Identifying small group possibilities is limited only by your imagination, but you shouldn't assume that "if you build it, they will come." Most of us are busy, and time constraints may prevent involvement even in groups we want to join. In any case, we don't usually join groups for superficial reasons. What does attract people to join groups?

- **We have something to offer.** The satisfaction of a job well done and appreciated by others can be a significant motivator. People who want and need an outlet to offer their gifts may welcome an invitation to join, even to lead, a new group. They may just be waiting to be asked.

- **We gain a sense of meaning or purpose.** In vocational arenas, tangible rewards may tie us to the desk or to the job but might not give us the sense that it really means anything. Christ-centered people will look for ways to invest their time in something that enables them to make meaning, advance the cause of Christ, or help others. Others may find an entry point for something needful that had been missing.

- **We gain a sense of belonging.** Active Christians typically will appreciate what it means to be part of the body of Christ and will find meaning and belonging with others who share that faith. Others who are yearning for or seeking community may find that sense of hospitality or kinship that had previously eluded them.

- **We get something we want or need.** We surely don't bother with groups in which we neither gain, nor give. The "something we want or need" could be a new skill, relational opportunity, outlet for a special interest, or support in difficult circumstances. Need is a powerful motivator, and strong internal urges will push us toward avenues of meeting needs, even if those needs are largely (or completely) unconscious.

Recruit and Prepare Leaders

New groups need leaders. You may identify new leaders during your discovery phase. You know not to grab the first person who offers or who is recommended without some further gifts discovery. Matching the gifts and abilities of a leader with the group he or she is asking to lead is crucial.

How do you get the leaders you need? Identify the gifts you need and the skill building you will offer and invite persons who have demonstrated those gifts. Notice and ask about persons who are spiritually and personally mature. Ask potential or current group members who they think would be a good leader. Inviting someone who has been asked for by name is very compelling. Survey current group members who have demonstrated initiative and leadership ability and ask if they would consider starting a new group (perhaps with a small core from their current group). Have a discernment and prayer session to see whose name emerges. Ask the church council members who they have observed to be potential leaders. Review notes taken at new member orientation to find out who has had leadership experience in another church. In addition, offer training in at least these basic leadership skills for all group leaders.

- **Listening to others:** staying engaged with the other person, processing what is being said, attending to what is behind the words, keeping track of body language; **listening to God:** through prayer, Scripture reading, and discerning with others; **listening to oneself:** checking instincts with assumptions, facts, and the response of others.

- **Communication skills:** clarity of thought and expression; speaking and listening respectfully and patiently; sensitivity to cultural differences, physical limitations, or other factors that have an impact on how another person should be addressed hospitably; avoiding pitfalls of interrupting, missing personal communication cues from others, invading the space of others while talking, talking too much or not enough.

- **People skills:** learning and using persons' names; sensitivity to feelings and special needs; respecting contributions to the group (even if they are not ultimately used); ability to build community and handle conflict; handling the differing personalities and needs of group members; keeping a sense of humor, not taking yourself too seriously, taking others seriously enough, and respecting others' time and other commitments.

- **Leadership skills:** balancing social and task demands and needs; managing time and meeting goals; helping group members identify their gifts and operate out of their strengths; using and sharing power to *empower*, not *overpower*; keeping the group on track with their vision and mission; being fair and just; building consensus and making appropriate decisions.

Start Up Stage

Following assessment, planning, and new leader recruitment and training, you are ready for the start up stage. Even though you are in the beginning stage, it is wise to also have the end in mind and to understand the group life cycle.

Small Group Life Cycle

The stages of group life begin with **birth** (the group is planned for, members identified); **formation** (members meet, begin to get acquainted with the purpose and with each other); **stability** ("all systems go"); **decline** (some loss of energy, focus, or vision); and **death** (group ends). Though described as a linear progression, the life cycle really is a dynamic cycle, not a line, and groups may move back and forth between stages or loop around completely from death to rebirth. ("Form → Storm → Perform → Norm" is another way to describe a group life cycle, but it does not account for "death.")

At birth, groups are in their infancy. Members may not know each other; the group vision and purpose are in their most initial stage. As the group forms, members develop trust and familiarity. They identify and agree upon certain expectations and commitments among themselves about how they will relate to one another and what they will do. This will happen, at least haphazardly, even if group members don't know it, so it's best to develop a covenant consciously and conscientiously. Covenants help group members define who they perceive God is calling them to be and what they are being called to do. As the group building occurs, as work toward group goals progresses, and as the group system falls into place, the group will stabilize. While this is naturally perceived as a good thing, stability could lead to complacency, a hidden danger.

Encourage and plan for dynamism; challenge group members to continue growing in multifaceted ways. Add new members, multiply groups, mentor new facilitators, move from short-term to longer-term studies, add a Bible study dimension, nurture the practice of the means of grace, introduce service or missional opportunities. This intentional growth plan will go a long way toward ensuring that social or other needs (which are OK) do not supersede the group's vision and stated purpose.

Nevertheless, if something deflects the group from its attention to its vision, the group will decline. If that deflection continues, the group may hang on for a long, long time, but eventually it will end. Those lingering deaths are painful, but not inevitable. Intervention or change at any of those transition points between stages will reshape the group.

Ideally, a group will keep itself in a loop of formation and stability. Anything that changes the configuration of the group (loss of members, new members, change of environment) pushes it into a formation stage, even if it has been stable and working effectively toward its vision and goals. As goals are accomplished, which can also shift the stability of a group, a healthy group will continue to identify new goals and will periodically review and update its vision. While the group works toward stability, it still remains fresh and forward-looking. In addition, healthy groups continually nurture and educate their leaders to re-energize them. Change in leadership is necessary and beneficial in many cases and will be another point of re-formation.

Without this constant renewal, groups will shift toward decline, so it becomes more urgent that the group "regroup." A group headed toward decline may require some kind of intervention, which could be a change of leadership, an insistent "wake up call" from a member, or request for evaluation from you or the church council. This gives the group another opportunity to re-examine its purpose, refine its goals and direction, and ask itself again what God's purpose is for that group at that particular time and place.

A group at the brink of death can still come back, but the change will probably be a drastic one, such as a large infusion of members, a relocation of their meeting space, or a shift to a new or different-but-related purpose. Incorporating one or more of these major changes will take the group back to the birthing stage. *As the small group ministries coordinator you will interpret this group life cycle to the small group leaders and help them maintain stable groups that keep themselves refreshed, renewed, and forward-looking.*

There is, of course, a big difference between ending a group that has completed its reason for being and either killing it off or letting it slip away. The assumption here is that groups we want to continue will need to be properly nourished so that they remain alive and vital.

Implementation Stage

At the implementation stage, you have done the congregational assessments, worked out a preliminary vision for an overall small group ministry and for specific new groups, understood the life cycle of group life and why people join groups, and identified and trained potential leaders. Again, these steps have been described sequentially, but most likely they will be in development concurrently; more than one thing will be happening at about the same time.

Interpretation

One of those steps is **interpretation.** Congregational members, and perhaps community members, will need to know what the small group landscape looks like in order to participate. Use whatever means are available to present this vision: church newsletter, bulletin boards, congregational letter, open house, fellowship or introductory dinner, brochure, phone tree—you are limited only by your imagination. Be sure to do this in cooperation with the church council.

- **Advertise all the groups already in existence and indicate what groups are open to new members and to what ages.** Some, such as a *Companions in Christ* group or DISCIPLE class, are closed for the duration but are repeated at regular intervals for new members. You can be sure that the existence of some of these groups will be news to some of your members. Part of the purpose of this notification is to help all your church members see the whole small group picture and the potential connections among the groups, even if not everyone will be a part of a group.

- **Publicize the potential groups that can start,** for what ages the groups are appropriate, and what the maximum number of members can be. One way to identify what groups to start is to ask persons what they want and need; even so, you don't have a group if you don't have members.

Potential group members will want to know who the group leader is, when the group meets first, for how long, for what purpose, and so on.

- **Seek information again about what groups may be needed that have not been planned for yet.** One way to sharpen this focus is to categorize the kinds of groups you have and what groups belong to those categories. (See the chart on page 13)

- **Encourage members to indicate their interest in particular groups,** using a congregational survey or sign-up sheet. Consider a small group fair with simple displays from each group and a way for members to sign on. Personal invitations will draw the greatest response, so enlist the help of those who have the engaging hospitality skills to invite and encourage others.

- **Ask the current and newly trained group leaders to gather to plan the best way to incorporate new members.** This is a time of excitement for new beginnings, but do remind them that some groups may founder, even with good leadership. Schedule a time (in two months and four months, for example) to assess how well groups are doing.

- **Invite persons to come to their first meetings**. Personal invitations are always a good idea, but group starts can also be publicized in the bulletin, on posters in high traffic areas, by e-mail, in the newsletter, and so on.

- **Give groups time to form;** to build up a sense of trust; to determine their covenant; to understand their biblical and theological reason for being; and to clarify their vision, purpose, and goals. After perhaps ten weeks, have group leaders evaluate what is going well and also what help they need in order to focus, organize, or care for one another. Encourage group leaders to challenge the group members to be honest about their feelings and desires for the continuation of the group. Keeping a group going just to have it going is a dishonor to the participants and to God. It is perfectly acceptable to disband, regroup, rethink goals, and start over.

- **Repeat the process**. New groups disband; new needs emerge; ongoing groups lose members. You will continue to need to assess the small group life, determine how to help ongoing groups that need help, end the groups that need to end, identify new persons who are not in small groups, assist persons who need to make a transition to a new or different group, and provide training and nurturing for current and potential new leaders.

Nurture Stage

The "ministry" of small group ministry is in equipping the group leaders to nurture their group members in faith formation so that they have a sense of their own discipleship. As the coordinator of small group ministries, you will monitor and evaluate the nurture phase for groups and group leaders. What are the elements of group nurture?

- **"Performing."** Group members build trust, establish a group covenant, tell the truth in love, and manage time wisely as they work toward their group's vision and mission.

- **Equipping group members for "everyday" ministry.** Group members see clearly their own gifts for ministry and how to live as faithful disciples in all aspects of daily life. They are empowered through good Christian practices and group dynamics skills. They continue to be formed in faith and to be held accountable in and with the community for their own growth.

- **Ongoing opportunities for refreshment.** Leaders and members will have available time for renewal through the practice of the means of grace, retreats or other time away, continuing education events, inspirational reading or speakers, or other development.

Ending Stage

Some groups have a natural life span, and their end is planned from the beginning, such as the task force planning this summer's camping event. Some ongoing groups that do short-term studies or programs may have a stable core group but gain and lose members at each change of study. Encourage groups to take stock periodically so that they remain in the "formation-stability" phase. The signs of the "decline-death" phase are usually obvious.

Signs of the End

- **Lack of participation.** Participants drop out or attend sporadically, don't stay on task; meetings are cancelled and perhaps not rescheduled; other covenant or accountability issues are ignored; members express boredom or lack of interest; the group has outlived its purpose; the group has not allowed for or planned for growth, so attrition slowly kills it.

- **Unhealthy participation.** Participants prefer to compete rather than cooperate, either with the leader or among themselves; one or more participants works to block or to sabotage the group efforts; confidences are not kept; group members are not honest, are uncaringly honest, or are dishonest; members are not supportive or will not be held accountable; one or more members (consciously or unconsciously) push their own agenda or needs at the expense of the group life or goals; members hang on to keep the group going without knowing or being able to state why.

- **No clear vision.** Participants have lost clear sight of their purpose; their original purpose was fulfilled and no new vision or purpose has replaced it; new members have not been oriented or came in with a different (perhaps unstated) vision in mind; personal needs or interests have slowly eroded or replaced the group goal with only social goals.

• **Diminished leadership:** The leader leaves without a replacement; does not have the vision to take the group where it expects to go; does not empower the participants to take responsibility or have a sufficient interest or stake in the group's goals; does not have sufficient skill to lead, resolve conflicts of personality or goals; has not dealt effectively with change.

To End or Not to End: Evaluation

What should you do when these (or other) signs mount up? Ideally, groups will evaluate their life together periodically and avoid crises of identity, purpose, or leadership. However, you will occasionally have to help group leaders who have reached an end stage. Consider these suggestions.

• **Remember the group life cycle** (see pages 24-25).

• **Review leadership.** A group tends to move in the direction of the leader's behavior. Is the leader going in the direction that the group and its purpose ought to go? Are there weaknesses in leadership that require re-tooling and nurture? Is a change in leadership indicated? Does the leader get sufficient support from group members, or is he or she left to carry all the group goals alone? Is the leader practicing the means of grace with the group?

• **Review vision and purpose.** What are the vision and mission of the group, and how well are they being carried out? Has anyone forgotten, tried to change, or actively rebelled against the group's vision or purpose? Has the purpose been fulfilled? How do the goals compare with the group's accomplishments? Does the focus need to change or the strategies to achieve the purpose? Does the group know its biblical and theological purpose and how it fulfills the primary task?

• **Examine practices for support and accountability.** How well are group members practicing support and accountability for the group covenant and for nurturing each other in faith and discipleship? Is this a group that would please God?

• **Identify who the stakeholders are and what is at stake for them**. Group members may have a wide variety of reasons for why a group is important to them, and those reasons may have little to do with the stated purpose of the group. Does the group meet crucial needs (from the participant's perspective) for community, belonging, purpose, power, exercise of gifts, control, identity, continuity, personal or family legacy, vocation, or tradition? Does someone outside the group use it obliquely for his or her own purposes and thus have a high need for the group to continue?

• **Consider your exit strategy.** If the group discontinues, what must first be in place? Is any approval required, and if so, by whom? Who is empowered to decide if the group can end and is that power shared as broadly as possible?

If minors are a part of the group, are they and their interests adequately cared for? Are there any covenantal, contractual, or legal obligations that must be satisfied? What financial issues have to be resolved and by whom? Is a new group needed to take its place? Is the group interconnected with any other group or person inside or outside the church that has to be involved in its ending? What courtesies should be extended to the stakeholders?

- **Give permission to stop when needed.** Group members may hold on without realizing that they don't have to, especially if the group has meant a lot to the participants and to the church or if closure is seen as "the end of an era." "Well done, good and faithful servant" may be just what members need to hear. (See the next point as well.)

- **Attend to issues of closure and pastoral care.** Never underestimate the power and necessity of ritual. We ritualize much of life because it is a way to bring order, make meaning, establish a context, and accord importance to what we do. Find appropriate ways to celebrate and say thank you, publicly and privately, to all participants. In an "end of an era" group, you might include past participants. If the closure of one group is the prelude to a new group, include persons on each side of the change.

  Surround these changes with plenty of prayer and personal contact. All changes, including welcome changes, open the possibility of grieving, so it is vital to offer appropriate care. Persons may require a break to recover or regroup, or they may be energized by the successful completion of one phase and be looking eagerly to the next. Work with group leaders to help them be sensitive to the kind of closure each participant will experience and work with your small group team to have suggestions for new groups or tasks for persons in transition. God always has something good in store for us.

- **Remember to do some "appreciative inquiry."** Throughout the evaluation, closure, and celebration, be sure to focus on what you appreciated about the group, its vision, its goals, and its accomplishments. If a group ends, especially on a disappointing or sour note, we may miss what excited the church and its members to engage in it in the first place. Recapturing those appreciated feelings, experiences, and successes will help invigorate you to carry on with the next vision, goals, and group.

Resources

Accountability and Covenant

• *Accountable Discipleship: Living in God's Household,* by Steven W. Manskar (Nashville: Discipleship Resources, 2000. ISBN 0-88177-339-5). A biblical, theological, and historical approach to accepting the challenge of personal discipleship for life.

• *Guide for Covenant Discipleship Groups,* by Gayle Turner Watson (Nashville: Discipleship Resources, 2000, 2001. ISBN 0-88177-305-0).

• *A Perfect Love: Understanding John Wesley's "A Plain Account of Christian Perfection,"* by Steven W. Manskar (Nashville: Discipleship Resources, 2004. ISBN 0-88177-388-3). An updated language version with study guide by Diana L. Hynson.

• *Guide for Class Leaders: A Model for Christian Formation,* by Grace Bradford (Nashville: Discipleship Resources, 1999, 2001. ISBN 0-88177-274-7).

• *Sprouts: Covenant Discipleship With Children,* by Edit Genung Harris and Shirley L. Ramsey (Nashville: Discipleship Resources, 2002. ISBN 0-88177-389-1).

• *Together in Love: Covenant Discipleship With Youth,* by David C. Sutherland (Nashville: Discipleship Resources, 1999. ISBN 0-88177-271-2). For youth leaders and campus ministers.

Christian Education and Formation

• *Keeping in Touch: Christian Formation and Teaching,* by Carol F. Krau (Nashville: Discipleship Resources, 1999. ISBN 0-88177-248-8). Processes for keeping in touch with God, God's people, one's own experience, the world, and teaching.

• *Synago* (Cokesbury). Small group resource series for senior highs, led by two student leaders and two adult "encouragers" for groups of up to eight.

Congregational Leadership

• *Equipped for Every Good Work: Building a Gifts-Based Church,* by Dan R. Dick and Barbara Miller (Nashville: Discipleship Resources, 2001. ISBN 0-88177-352-2). A process for gift discovery, spirituality types, interaction styles, and working preferences.

• *Faithful Leadership: Learning to Lead With Power,* by Thomas R. Hawkins (Nashville: Discipleship Resources, 1999. ISBN 0-88177-253-4). Biblical and sociological principles of servant leadership with practical advice.

- *FaithQuest: A Journey Toward Congregational Transformation,* by Dan R. Dick (Nashville: Discipleship Resources, 1998, 2002. ISBN 0-88177-399-9). Seventeen-week study to help form Christ-centered churches.

Group Process

- *Group Dynamics* (third edition), by Donelson R. Forsyth (Wadsworth Publishing, 1998. ISBN 0534-261-485).

- *Facilitating With Ease,* by Ingrid Bens (Jossey-Bass, 2000. ISBN 0-787-951-943). Description of facilitation for small group leaders.

History, Theology, and Spirituality

- *Eight Life Enriching Practices of United Methodists,* by Henry H. Knight, III (Nashville: Abingdon Press, 2001. ISBN 0-687-08734-1). Basic practices necessary for Christian formation.

- *The Soul of Tomorrow's Church: Weaving Spiritual Practices in Ministry Together,* by Kent Ira Groff (Nashville: Upper Room Books, 2000. ISBN 0-835-809-277).

- *Staying Focused: Building Ministry Teams for Christian Formation,* by M. Anne Burnette Hook and Shirley F. Clement (Nashville: Discipleship Resources, 2002. ISBN 0-88177-295-X). Focus on spiritual formation of the members of various ministry teams.

- *The Wesleyan Tradition: A Paradigm for Renewal,* edited by Paul W. Chilcote (Nashville: Abingdon Press, 2002. ISBN 0-687-09563-8). A collection of essays that describe the basic theology and practices of Christian formation in the Wesleyan tradition.

Small Group Ministry

- *Cultivating Christian Community,* by Thomas R. Hawkins (Nashville: Discipleship Resources, 2001. ISBN 0-88177-327-1). Describes the marks of Christian community in small groups, accountability groups, service groups, support groups, and administrative groups. Also available for Lay Speaking training.

- *The Christian Small-Group Leader,* by Thomas R. Hawkins (Nashville: Discipleship Resources, 2001. ISBN 0-88177-328-X). Helps group leaders form and transform a people of God.

- *Building and Growing Your Small-Group Ministry,* by Judith M. Bunyi (Nashville: Discipleship Resources, 2002. ISBN 0-88177-321-2). Biblical, theological, historical, and sociological foundations for small groups.

- *The Heart's Journey: Christian Spiritual Formation in the Life of a Small Group,* by Barb Nardi Kurtz (Nashville: Discipleship Resources, 2001. ISBN 0-88177-326-3). Weaving the means of grace in the life of your small group.